KANTIS SIMMONS

SCHOLARSHIP SECRETS REVEALED

The Roadmap to Locate, Land and Lockdown Free College Funding

TO:______________________________

FROM:____________________________

ISBN: 978-0-9767812-3-3
SIMMONS, KANTIS
SCHOLARSHIP SECRETS REVEALED

Legal & Disclaimer

The content and information in this book are consistent and truthful, and it has been provided for informational, educational, and business purposes only.

The content and information in this book have been compiled from reliable sources, which are accurate based on the author's knowledge, belief, expertise, and communication.

The author cannot be held liable for omissions and errors.

TABLE OF CONTENTS

0 INTRODUCTION 1

1 THE "**F**": FOCUS ON YOUR FUTURE 5

2 THE "**U**": UNDERSTAND THE PROCESS 13

3 THE "**N**": NAME YOUR GOAL 33

4 THE "**D**": DEVELOP YOUR PLAN 49

5 THE "**I**": INITIATE THE PROCESS 75

6 THE "**N**": NAIL DOWN SCHOLARSHIPS 103

7 THE "**G**": GET AND KEEP THE MONEY 125

NEXT STEPS 135

INTRO

Introduction

Deciding on a career is one thing, but having a map of how to reach that goal is yet another puzzle.

For many people, their map to achieving their life's purpose is following the road called "college".

But most people often get either overwhelmed or downright discouraged for different reasons.

Out of those many reasons, there is the issue of what course to take and especially how to get funding without incurring debt.

When people mention scholarships as a way out of that, everyone gets excited, at least for a while.

But after some time, myths and half-truths start to wage war on people's confidence and enthusiasm about going to college.

It is because of these reasons I have created this resource.

I understand the unique place of guidance when raising funds for college and all the other details.

Welcome to "Scholarship Secrets Revealed," your guide to navigating the often confusing and intimidating world of funding your higher education.

As you embark on this journey, it's important to remember that you are not alone. Many people struggle with figuring out how to pay for college and worry about taking on student debt. That's where this book comes in.

In these pages, you'll find all the information you need to understand the process of seeking, finding, and securing scholarships to fund your education.

Whether you're just starting to consider college or you're well on your way to earning your degree, this book is here to support you every step of the way.

We'll go over the myths and half-truths that can hold you back and provide you with the knowledge and confidence you need to succeed.

Using the acronym "F.U.N.D.I.N.G." we'll cover everything from focusing on your future to nailing down that scholarship and everything in between.

So, get ready to dive in and start your path to funding your higher education with confidence and success.

CHAPTER 1: THE "F"

FOCUS ON YOUR

FUTURE

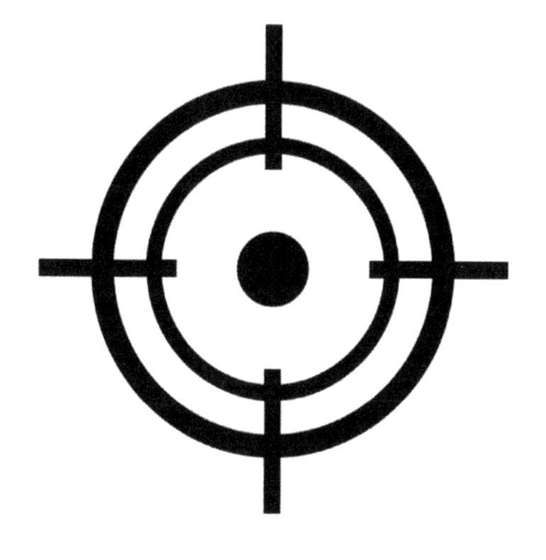

Chapter 1 – The "F"
FOCUS ON YOUR FUTURE

It's natural for humans to look towards a better future and to have aspirations for what we want our lives to be. From a young age, we're encouraged to imagine and plan for our future goals.

However, as we grow older, we may encounter two different realities. Some of us may have a clear vision of the life we want and work towards achieving it, while others may face challenges such as poverty, lack of resources, illness, and illiteracy.

Regardless of what reality we find ourselves in, it's essential to have a clear idea of what we want for our future and a plan for how to achieve it. This can act as a compass, guiding us toward the life we envision for ourselves and helping us to make it a reality.

Regarding education, it's essential to start by thinking about what you truly desire. This might be a specific degree, a certain career path, or a particular institution. Take some time to consider what truly excites you and what you want to achieve through your education.

Once you have a clear idea of what you want, it's time to focus on the process of achieving it. This might include researching schools and programs, filling out applications, and applying for financial aid or scholarships. It's important to be organized and proactive in this process, as it will help you stay on track and reach your goals.

Overall, it's important to remember that your education is a journey, and it's up to you to chart the course. With the right combination of desire and focus on the process, you can achieve your educational dreams and reach your goals.

So, to get started in this section, there are two things that you should focus on:

1. Your Desire

2. The Process

When it comes to motivation, what comes to mind for you? For me, the word "move" immediately comes to mind. This leads to the following questions:

- What inspires you to take action?
- What drives you to succeed?
- What are your aspirations and goals?
- What will help you reach the next level?
- Why do you want to go to college?
- What major will best support your career goals?

When it comes to choosing a college major, there are a few things to consider. Here are some suggestions:

Begin with Your Destination In Mind

Look into the future! You have identified and thought about the definite thing you want to do in the future. You may have researched what major you will need and what careers are out there.

Now, you want to continue researching. I think it's a hard thing when you go into a specific field and don't do your research. Then, you look up years later and realize there isn't a career in that field. To avoid this, you need to do your research.

What do 2024, 2025, and 2026 look like? What does 2030 look like? If you can predict some things, I want you to be prepared. Avoid over-specializing; don't get trapped. Here's what I mean by this. Sometimes, you can go to a specific school to get a certain degree, and you are so overspecialized that, when you need to make a shift, you can't because you only know only that one thing.

I think about football players or people who graduate high school early or don't finish college degrees. Then, they say, "You know what? I want to be a football player." That’s cool, but what happens if you get injured? You're so overspecialized in football that you wouldn’t be able to make a shift if you needed to. Don't get trapped.

Or you have somebody who says, "Hey, I want to do this and nothing but this, and I'm so focused on this." It’s essential not to overspecialize when looking at a particular major. When deciding on a major, you want to review all of the prerequisites you may need to get into that program.

I will share further details with you on building your future by following the process and procedure required.

USE THIS AREA TO JOT SOME NOTES AND YOUR ACTIVE CURRENT THOUGHTS ABOUT THIS SECTION

CHAPTER 2: THE "U"

UNDERSTAND THE PROCESS

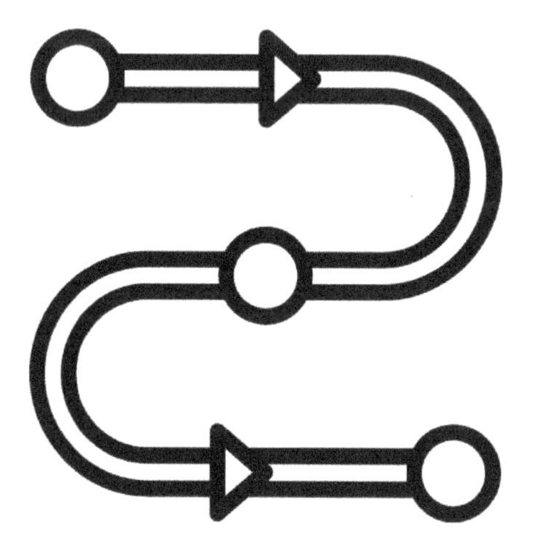

Chapter 2 – The "U"
UNDERSTAND THE PROCESS

One of the most typical mistakes people make when building a future for themselves is that they only stop at identifying their major.

It is not enough to know what you want to do.

Knowing what you want to do should propel you to take steps to do it.

So, in this chapter, I will take you through the understanding of the processes you've got to follow.

Yes, you have defined the desire and identified the major, with details on the program. If not, you can go on the internet and look at the programs that the schools offer.

Some colleges have outstanding business programs. Within those business programs, they may have specializations in accounting and finance, insurance, marketing, real estate, etc. This college may have a great program in the school of business, but it is a poor science program.

Now, the challenge is that you want to major in chemistry, but you're going to a college that has a firm business program offer.

Moreover, you may be going to a school that is strong in science and, engineering, medicine and is a technological leader in the university system at the same time. But you want to major in sociology. That would benefit you, or would it?

The recommendation is that you should not pick a college because of its name or prestige. Instead, choose the college because of the program.

I need you to understand that you should not choose a college because of its reputation but because of the program. Therefore, you want to research the programs that are being offered.

Now, you want to go through the **search process**.

I like a few cars: the BMW X6, the Mercedes Benz GLE, and the Bentley Truck.

These fantastic cars are designed to get their driver from point A to point B.

Think about how selective you are when searching for a car.

You want to test-drive it, right?

When you decide on a car, a house, a prom dress, or a mate, you're going to spend some time researching.

So, search for a college the same way you would for a car.

Search for a college the same way you would search for a house.

Look for a college the same way you would search for a mate.

You don't want to get into a relationship and marry just anybody. You take some time to research and collect data…some people call it dating.

Well, the same is true for a college. You're going to have to search it out.

- Does it fit?

- Does it have what you desire?

- Does it look the way you want it to look?
- Does it provide the resources and give you the skills needed to be successful?
- Do you enjoy the comfort of it?
- Does that college brand line up with your brand?

So, searching for a college is the same as searching for a mate or a car.

Here are a few things you want to know where colleges are concerned about when searching.

Some of these phrases are going to pop up. When you hear or see these keywords or phrases during your search process, it may cause you to make some adjustments.

One word is **selectivity,** measured by the admitted students' percentage. What does selectivity mean? The lower the selectivity percentage, the more selective the school.

A small group of highly selective schools admits less than a third of all applicants. So, when you're looking for a college, you want to ask yourself,

“Should I spend my time in this college, knowing that they can be highly selective?"

That selective percentage is going to be low. For instance, if one hundred people apply to the college, they’re only going to select three out of that hundred. But with your research, you know what your percentage is and how their percentage looks, and you look at the probability of getting in there.

Here are some other things you want to consider when figuring out which college is for you.

- Are you comfortable being yourself while also being challenged to be better?

Sometimes you can go to a school, like, "Eh, this is too easy." You're not challenged.

When selecting a college, consider if it is right for you - for example, if you…

- Can you find people to talk to (or study with) incredibly late into the night?

Again, it could be right for you because you agree with each other or you're debating something you care about.

- Does the college campus become a ghost town when the sun goes down?
- Are there opportunities to study things that fascinate you?
- Can you play the sports you have skills in?
- Can you work at internships that help you?
- Does this college give you opportunities?

When thinking about selecting a college, you must consider all these factors.

Here are a few more things to consider when deciding which college is a good fit for you.

- Will you learn how to communicate well?
- Will you learn how to learn?
- Will you learn how to solve problems?

- Will you learn skills employers want to see, regardless of the industry?

- Can you get the education you need without breaking the bank and taking on excessive student loan debt?

Here are some things to avoid when choosing a college.

1. **First**, avoid rushing into making a decision.

2. **Second**, avoid being a follower.

3. **Third**, avoid choosing a college just because of legacy. "my mother went to this school, my uncle went to this school, my grandmother and grandfather went to this school, so I have to attend." That's not a good reason to choose a college. It may have some perks. But will it give you what you need?

4. The **fourth** thing to avoid is rebellion. Meaning, "Man, I don't want to go to

this college because it's right down the street" or "I don't want to go to this college because it's in-state. I want to go to my dream school." You rebel against this great opportunity, attending this particular school, even though the money is there. Just avoid it as best as you can.

5. **Fifth**, avoid choosing a college because you're a die-hard fan. Look, I was a big Clemson University fan while growing up. I loved Clemson football. As a child, I would get little white football helmets and paint them like Clemson University helmets. I wanted to go to Clemson just because of the football team, but I didn't count the cost. I didn't look at everything that went on there.

6. **Sixth**, avoid the temptation to party. Fine, all colleges have parties. Well, except maybe the online schools. They may have virtual parties. I don't know. But you want to avoid these mistakes.

7. Avoid focusing on how a student's body looks. You may think, "Oh, the people over here look a certain way." Please, don't make that mistake.

8. Also, you may want to watch your expectations. Avoid assuming that the worst will happen.

9. Regarding location, please don't make the mistake of choosing a college solely based on its location. You think it's right down the street, so I need to go there. It may be down the road, but they may not have the program to help you in your future career.

10. Avoid carelessness and costly obsession. You can do better than making careless decisions and choosing to go to the wrong college.

11. Another mistake you should avoid is deciding not to visit the college. Every college looks good on the internet. Every college seems reasonable on the brochures you're getting in the mail.

Please take a tour of the colleges. Don't rely solely on reputation. Harvard could sound nice; Yale could be known as outstanding, and UCLA is famous. To find out for yourself. You talk to people. For parents, please do not coerce your kids to go to a particular college because you want them to. As a family, I want you guys to sit down and examine the pros and cons.

12. Avoid having a one-track mind just because the college specializes in your current major. Remember, overspecialization can put you in a bind. So, all of these are mistakes you should avoid.

Another thing you want to consider is location.

Now, you understand what you have going on and where the site is concerned.

At one time, I thought about leaving Decatur, Georgia, and going to California because I am from the Atlanta area and wanted something different.

But once I started thinking about it, I was like, "Wait a minute. I can't drive home."

I don't have any family over there. If I wanted to come home, it would be a four-hour flight to Atlanta and a four-hour flight back. If I wanted my family (dad, mom, brother, and sister) to visit, they would need to purchase four tickets to Cali and four back.

If I'd had an emergency, there would not have been anybody who could get to me within a few hours, so location is important.

- Do you want to attend in-state or out-of-state?
- How far out of state are you willing to want to go?
- Do you want to be in the city or the country?

This is not to make a disparaging remark: I love my HBCUs (historically black colleges and universities).

Man, I visited Tuskegee University once, and it was deep, profoundly, deep in the country.

I realized that was not for me.

...so, location is critical for you to consider when looking at colleges.

The next thing you want to consider is the application.

This is all part of the process. What's the best way to submit your college application?

One of the terms you will hear when applying is **regular admissions**. This is the most common option for four-year colleges and universities.

All students must submit their applications by a specific date, usually between November and January.

The admissions board then reviews all the applications and sends out acceptance and rejection letters on the same day.

Another term is **rolling admissions**.

Commonly used at more prominent state universities, this term refers to the process that allows students to apply at any time during the admissions period. This typically runs from September to July.

The school then evaluates each college application received and sends acceptance letters to students who meet their requirements. Since admission is granted on a first-come, first-served basis, you may have to submit your application as early as possible.

Next, there are **open admissions** typically offered by community colleges, online schools, and distance learning programs. This type of enrollment means that the school admits nearly all high school graduates provided they have a diploma, a GED (General Education Diploma), or a development program certificate.

Students with a lower-than-average GPA in their high school courses may want to find a college with this policy. Online schools are a great alternative to further your education if there's no community college in your area that matches your interest. Schools that offer open admissions can take in anyone willing and able.

Under an **early decision admissions** program, you agree to attend a particular school if accepted. You cannot apply to any other college or university. If you receive an acceptance letter from an early-decision school, you must withdraw all applications to any other schools.

Since this option is binding, you must be sure about your choice and realistic about your application. Ensure you get your guidance counselor's opinion before submitting an early decision application. Hopefully, you understand that.

Some schools have an early decision admissions process, and you agree to attend that school. Whether it's with a letter of intent or verbal intent, you agree to go to this school and withdraw your application from any other school.

Next, there's **early action**, similar to early decision, in that you apply only to your top-choice school. However, unlike early decisions, you are not bound to attend if accepted. You can apply early action to more than one university. Also, you can take an offer as soon as you receive it or wait to make your final selection in the spring after you've found out where else you've been accepted.

Here's one more **early evaluation**. Selecting this choice means applying early to determine whether your chances for acceptance are reasonable, fair, or poor. Your application usually needs to be submitted by November, after which you'll be sent a determination letter by December or January.

This is a way of testing the waters to see if you can get into a specific school. It is also a way to see if the possibility of your getting accepted is poor, fair, or reasonable. Hence the term early evaluation.

So, those are several different ways to apply.

Here's something you can do right now. **Get those grades up, starting today.**

No one wants to buy an ugly truck. If your grades are low, do whatever needs to be done to get your grades up immediately.

For juniors, get your grades up.

Seniors, you need to close the year out strong. If you're currently in college, get those grades up.

If you need help with your grades and academic performance, I encourage you to get access to my book, Play Your 'A' Game.

It will show you how to stay motivated, remain focused, and succeed in school and life.

(You can get access to the book at KantisSimmons.com*)*

Invest in getting those grades up.

Maybe you have a few people who would buy an ugly truck, like Fred Sanford back in the day. But, typically, nobody wants to invest in an ugly truck, right?

Here's what you can do now…

Fill out the applications. You can't win the lottery if you don't buy a ticket. You can't be accepted to a college if you do not fill out the application. You cannot go to your dream school if you've never looked into the requirements for admissions you've never looked into applying.

Here's another thing you can do now…

Get recommendations and write your essays for those college applications. Then, you can recycle and reuse those. We're going to talk more about that later on. But if a teacher gives you a recommendation and you can use it for multiple schools, then go ahead and use it. If you write an essay that can be used for numerous school applications, use it. Recycle and reuse those, also.

If you have the opportunity to interview with the school, or you have the chance to talk to them one-on-one, let your light shine. Put your best foot forward in letting your personality and passion into the interview.

Smile in your essays. Understand that real people with real emotions are reading them.

When you write your college essay, stay away from sad memories that make you cry, type of essays.

Suppose you go low emotionally on your essays. Know how to lift the reader back up and smile with your essays.

So, where are you and your household in this process?

- Have you decided about the top 5 or 10 schools to which you want to apply?
- Have you applied to any schools?
- Have you started researching?
- Have you researched the school's programs?
- Where are you in the process?

USE THIS AREA TO JOT SOME NOTES AND YOUR ACTIVE CURRENT THOUGHTS ABOUT THIS SECTION

CHAPTER 3: THE "N"

NAME YOUR

GOAL

Chapter 3 – The "N"
NAME YOUR GOAL

Let's discuss the "N" in F-U-N-D-I-N-G.

I want you to consider your goals and the importance of narrowing things down.

As a student or a parent, how you name your goal and visualize the plan is key to funding your college education.

Let's say you're considering 5 to 10 schools. Here are four things to think about:

1. What do you want to be?

2. What do you want to see?

3. What do you want to do?

4. What do you want to have?

Visualize how you're going to get there. Think about those goals, then take some time to write them down. Write the vision and make it plain.

As a family, get together and discuss your goals. As a parent, consider the big goal for your student. As a student, what’s the big goal for your academic career? What's the goal for the family?

Honestly, my dad and I just had a conversation probably last year. I brought him on a podcast episode, and I was like, "How come you and I never talked about college? We never talked about what you and Mama had put aside. Why didn't we take the time to talk about that?"

The thought that motivated me was this, “I'm from a middle-class, broke family. I don't know what they have lined up for money.”

We didn't have a conversation. But then he told me, just a year ago, "You know your mom and I had plans for you. We just wanted you to focus on your grades."

Interestingly, that's what I did…

We never talked about “MONEY,” and I was never really sure what they had planned or what money they had stored up. I was like, “Hey, I'm about to go out here and look for these scholarships.”

Whether it's a band scholarship, a baseball scholarship, a glee club scholarship, or a music scholarship, we never had a goal, and we never talked about the plan.

That's the thing I want you to see and understand. As a household, are you in one accord?

This is why writing the goal and making it simple is crucial.

What is the vision?

The logic is to see your goal, say your destination, and declare your plan.

Studies have shown that individuals who write, see and declare their goals daily are 80% closer to accomplishing them. They are more apt to achieve their goals than people who don't set them.

What am I saying? Think about the plan and where you want to be. I want you to write them down and to see them. Put it on the refrigerator, the bathroom mirror, in the kitchen, and even on your phone.

I want you to start declaring it. Put the phrase "I am" in front of everything you want to accomplish.

I want you to state your goal in the present tense. Here are some examples:

- "I am ___________."
- "I am happily enjoying a degree from Clemson University."
- "I am happily enjoying graduating from Howard University, debt-free."
- "I'm happily enjoying a career in medicine."
- "I happily just paid my last payment for college."
- "I am out of college debt."
- "I am enjoying my business and the fruits of my labor."
- "I am in love with my spouse, and our kids are happy in college."

What's the goal?

Wherever you may be, I want you to write it. Write out your "I am" statements for your family.

Go ahead, take some time to visualize, and declare the goal.

See it and write it down. It may not be happening right now, but imagine it anyway.

- “I am graduating debt-free.”
- “I am debt-free for all three daughters in college.”
- “My son is graduating from college, debt-free.”
- “I am enjoying life, debt-free.”
- “I'm in college on a full ride.”
- “I'm sending my son to Berkeley College of Music, debt-free.”
- “I am on track to graduate from my high school with a 4.2 GPA and a capstone diploma.”
- “I’m graduating, debt-free, from SCAD. Look, make it present tense.”

Avoid saying something like "graduated," say, "I am graduating," or "I'm a graduate of SCAD, debt-free."

Make it present-tense, and make it super-clear.

For example, “I am happily married to my husband, and we’re the proud parents of three debt-free college graduates.”

- “I'm working a job that I love and am using my college as a stepping stone to get there.”
- “I am debt-free for college degrees for my daughters and finishing my college degree programs.”
- “My children are debt-free and building generational wealth.”

Do you feel that? Do you think you were empowered a little bit? It's like something that makes you know you have a vision. This could be a reality.

This is good stuff.

I wish I had somebody to encourage me like this.

I want you to understand it.

Even after you read this, I want you to name this goal and write it down. You put it up so the whole family can see it, and you guys talk about it.

Next, I want you to reverse your goal or work the plan backward. Let me show you how to reverse your goal.

Here's how most people approach their goals. Most people live life in the unknown. That means, "I don't know what tomorrow will bring. I'm not sure what the future looks like."

So, you're taking steps by faith. You're stepping out, moving towards something without knowing what that something is. You're moving forward into the unknown.

Here is what I believe...

And this is not a teaching on the law of attraction, manifestation, or anything like that. Here is just how

I've seen the system work. And I study people; they teach this principle a lot, and it just works.

Please think about it.

Rather than just walking forward blindly, I want you to do it this way. I want you to live life this way. Rather than walking into the unknown, I want you to start here with your goal.

Now, you've already declared your goal.. The goal is to graduate debt-free.

Let's take our minds to that goal and work backward.

So you want to be a debt-free graduate?

Let's go ahead and see ourselves at the graduation.

...Oh, I'm about to graduate in a few weeks.

...That means you are a senior.

....As a senior, you went somewhere,

Now, you work backward. What happened before senior year?

…Oh, I was a junior, and I had an internship.

…Before that internship, I spent time in the Chemistry laboratory working on a research project with my advisor and had a fellowship. And because of my Chemistry degree, my advisor had me on scholarship.

..I met my advisor at a recruiting fair. A

…And before that, I read the book College Paid in Full, written by this cool guy named Kantis, who helped my family.

So, now, what we're doing is reversing the process.

Whereas before we walked forward, I now want us to walk backward.

Create it backward.

Let's reverse our goals backward.

Let's visualize our goals already done.

Then, let's reverse engineer the process of being at our dream school!

It's all about being able to reverse engineer the process. You have to come to grips with your goals.

- What's the college, the career, the life you want?
- What college do you like to attend?
- What kind of life do you want to live?
- Do you want to be single or married? Do you want two kids, four kids, or no kids?
- Do you want to live in California?
- Do you want to live in Europe?
- Do you want to live in Jamaica?
- What kind of career do you want?
- How much do you want to make?

Now that you can see it - college, career, life, you can visualize it and say it.

Now, let's reverse-engineer it.

- Hey, what are you wearing to that graduation?

- What's your job going to look like after graduation?

That is because you're going to graduate.

- You're having a graduation party, so do you imagine you paid back your student loan debt?
- Did you get all the scholarships you wanted and apply for the scholarships?

See it and work it backward.

Think, write, say, and reverse your goals.

That is the third thing there. **Name your goal.**

CHAPTER 4: THE "D"

DEVELOP YOUR

PLAN

Chapter 4 – The "D"
DEVELOP YOUR PLAN

In this section, I will talk about "D," which stands for developing your plan.

I have created a three-step framework for funding your college education

The equation talks about the big goal of paying for college.

The equation is GM + OM + YM.

If it costs $41,000 a year, or whatever that number is for your college, GM + OM + YM is the formula to come up with the $41,000

What is GM?

GM is getting access to the government's money.

Some reports show that $2.7 billion of federal funds go unclaimed.

That's right, $2.7 billion go unclaimed because high school graduates and college-bound students don't apply for it.

Resources are out there, but people need to apply for them.

I firmly believe that if you don't have money for college, your #1 goal should be looking for money for college.

Seek college funds now, or pay for college with your own money.

Your number one goal should be seeking out money.

Here's the reality…

…you will not always be in this season of your life. So, you must take the time to do just that, to apply.

Now, how do we get access to the government's money?

The number one way is through FAFSA, also known as the Free Application for Federal Student Aid.

Now, if you need money to pay for college this year, I hope you have already applied for FAFSA. (the updated federal student aid website is studentaid.gov.) or google "FAFSA" to find the most updated website.

There are some things you want to do to apply, but it begins with your FAFSA process by creating a federal student aid ID at fafsa.gov.

It's your code for submitting the FAFSA when you're ready.

Your FAFSA ID will give you access to the FSA online systems and can serve as your legal signature.

When you log in, the student must have access, and the parent must have access; therefor, they both need an ID.

The federal student aid application will be submitted starting October 1st, for most states, at the website.

Federal financial aid is awarded on a first-come, first-served basis. So, know your deadlines and apply as early as possible to maximize your financial support.

When it comes to deadlines, you must think locally. Colleges and state financial aid deadlines vary by state.

If you go to the website, you can find the state's financial assistance deadline. My recommendation is for you to apply for FAFSA annually and early.

You must fill out the FAFSA each year that you need money or plan to be a student.

Schools use the FAFSA to put together your financial aid package for one year of college, not the entire four years. It's just for one year.

That means you have to take time to go in and do this every single year.

So, how do we file the FAFSA to get federal student aid?

Here are some things you want to do to gather all the necessary information.

You need your:

- driver's license,

- social security number,
- parent's social security number, and
- birth dates.

You'll need…

- your family's latest federal income tax returns.

For example, if you are applying for financial aid for the academic year 2021-2022, you'll likely use your family's 2020 tax returns.

Now, if you don't have your taxes done for 2020, go ahead and put the 2019 return in there.

When you update your taxes, the good thing is that your tax returns and your FAFSA are linked. So, in some cases, it will automatically update with the FAFSA application.

You'll also need

- your W2 forms,
- bank statements, and
- information on your family's investments,

- real estate,
- money market funds,
- stocks, et cetera.

You should bookmark the website (https://studentaid.gov/) on your computer because this is where you get your federal student aid ID and submit the FAFSA application.

Make sure you pay attention to avoid falling for the scams out there.

The only site you should use to fill out FAFSA is the official website.

Understand that there is no charge for submitting the FAFSA. It's a FREE application.

Once you go to it, it also has the most up-to-date information on upcoming changes.

The easiest and fastest way is to file the FAFSA online with your FSA ID.

Your federal student aid ID is made up of your username and password.

Your application should be processed within three to five days.

You can mail a paper application, but the process will take longer - about seven to ten days.

Many people don't use paper applications. You can still get one, but ideally, you want to do it online.

Now, the FAFSA form will calculate your "EFC". That's an Expected Financial Contribution number.

The Expected Family Contribution (EFC) is a measure of your family's financial strength. Your EFC is calculated according to a formula established by law.

The formula considers your family's taxed and untaxed income, assets, and benefits (such as unemployment or Social Security).

The formula also considers your family size and the number of family members who will attend college during the year.

We use the information you report on your Free Application for Federal Student Aid (FAFSA®) form to calculate your EFC. Schools use the EFC to determine your federal student aid eligibility and financial aid award.

You can find your EFC on the first page of your Student Aid Report (SAR).

Note: Your EFC is not the amount your family will have to pay for college, nor is it the federal student aid you will receive. It is a number that schools use to calculate the amount of federal student aid you are eligible to receive.

The federal method, EFC calculation, takes into consideration four main areas, two of which are: parent income and parent assets. This does not include retirement funds, home equity, or small family businesses with under 100 employees. It also takes into consideration student income and student assets.

Example calculations

Here are three examples of how this calculation will work:

- Imagine your EFC is $15,000. At a school where the COA (Cost of Attendance) is $30,000, your calculated financial need is $30,000 (COA) – $15,000 (EFC) = $15,000 (Financial Need).

- Imagine your EFC is $22,000. At a school where the COA is $30,000, your calculated financial need is $30,000 (COA) – $22,000 (EFC) = $8,000 (Financial Need).

- Imagine your EFC is $22,000, but now you're attending a school where the COA is $18,000. Since your EFC is greater than your COA, your calculated financial need is $0, and you would not receive any financial aid. (Your family can afford to pay more than the college costs.)

As you can tell, given the same COA, a lower EFC generally means more financial aid. However, it's all relative since these numbers are in relation to each other.

Maximizing your Financial Aid Returns

You may have achieved some results already and may be thinking, "I don't like the results I received."

In that case, here are some things you can do to maximize that return:

1. M*inimize your capital gains*

Minimize your capital gains because any capital gains realized from January of the junior year and throughout your child's sophomore year in college will be treated as income in your FAFSA calculation.

If possible, offset any capital gains with losses to afford to increase your AGI. Were any money or payments that came in between your child's junior year and their sophomore year in college? If so, see what you can do to minimize those capital gains.

2. *Keep your IRA or 401(k) intact*

Do not withdraw money from an IRA or 401(k) unless it's taxable income within the financial aid calculation, which now reduces next year's financial aid eligibility. If you must use your retirement funds, borrow the money from the retirement fund instead of getting a distribution. Different circumstances apply to Roth IRAs. Do not withdraw money from the IRA or your 401(k).

3. ***Contribute to your retirement fund***

Maximize contributions to your retirement fund before the tax year ending in December of your student's 10th-grade year. Retirement savings and 401(k) accounts are shielded from the FAFSA formula. But retirement contributions made during the FAFSA and the years applying for financial aid are considered income within the calculation of financial assistance.

4. ***Save money in your name and not your kids' name.***

Another crucial step is to maximize retirement savings before your kids get to December of their sophomore year in high school. This is something that the department has taught me and has shared with me; some things that you can do. Save money in the parent's name, not the child's name, or move money in the student's name to the parent's name before the second semester, junior year of high school.

FAFSA assesses the parent's assets at 5.64% versus 20% for assets in the student's name. So, if there's something that you have in the student's name and you can move it, do that. Move it out of the child's name and into the parent's name.

5. ***Pay off Debt you can handle***

Compare your cost of money and evaluate if you have consumer debt such as credit cards, auto-loan balances, or a mortgage that you can consider paying off. Look at your assets; at the amount of debt out of the things that you owe. If you can pay something off, go ahead! Put savings in a 529 college savings plan and a 529 college payment plan. Make out your contributions each year. All immediate family 529 plans are considered parental assets.

6. ***Spend the students' assets and income***

Assets at the maximum rate of 5.64% and distributions have no impact on financial aid eligibility. Spend down the student's assets and income first. If you have money in your child's name that you can't move away from, it's better to use your student's assets to pay for all college expenses first.

Then, in subsequent years, parent assets will be assessed at a lower rate of 5.6% rather than 20%. If you don't qualify for any financial aid because your EFC is too high, it may be better to keep the money in your child's name for tax purposes. You can talk to a CPA more about this. You know where your money's going. You know what you have involved there.

7. ***Don't delay necessary expenses.***

Next, accelerate necessary expenses to reduce available cash. For example, if you need a new car or a computer, buy it before you file the FAFSA. If you don't qualify for financial aid, this may not apply because your EFC is too high. If you are considering purchasing a car, compare the car loan cost to a parent PLUS loan. If you're going to get a loan for a vehicle vs. a loan for a parent, consider the timing, then go ahead and accelerate those things before completing FAFSA.

8. ***Get two or more kids enrolled in college at a go***

Plan to have two or more children in college at the same time. There are benefits to having two or more kids in college simultaneously if you can. It sounds crazy to want to have two children in college simultaneously, but this will significantly increase their financial aid eligibility.

Your family is responsible for the total EFC. Most colleges will make allowances for knowing that a family simultaneously has more than one student in college. Many will reduce the family's total EFC by the number of students in college.

So, each student has an EFC that is half the total if there are two children. With this in mind, it may make sense to have one student wait so that you can have two siblings enrolled simultaneously. You know where your kids lie. Maybe they're two or three years apart. If they ever get to that place, there's some benefit to having those two kids.

9. How Grandparents Can Contribute

Consider the implications of how grandparents give money to help pay for college. There are several approaches that grandparents, aunts, and uncles can take if they would like to help save and pay for college. The implications depend upon what schools the student chooses to apply to and if the student may be eligible for aid. To be safe, it's best to contribute to a 529 plan rather than have it in the parent's name.

Another option is for grandparents to pay for the last two years of college or help pay off the loans after the student has graduated. Often, grandparents give money to the kids, and kids have all this money stored up.

What you can potentially do is have the grandparents, aunts, and uncles who contribute, put the funds into a 529 plan. Or have them hold onto that money and pay it toward the student loan. So, those are tips for you. Hopefully, these are helpful.

Here are a few other things to consider,..

10. Move the money, and here's why.

When the department of education reviews your income, assets, and family information, it will come up with a figure known as your EFC. That's your Expected Family Contribution.

The EFC is how much money you are supposed to be able to pay toward college expenses. So, the college you attend will use the EFC figure to determine how much aid you get. If you can move the money around, do so wisely. If you can use cash to pay down debt, use it.

Having debt like credit cards or car loans doesn't reduce your eligibility for financial aid, but having cash does—standard advice: pay down debt and make big purchases before filing a FAFSA.

If you have a lot of savings, consider spending some of those savings on paying off your debt. This has the primary advantage of reducing your EFC, the asset base by which your need is assessed. Also, watch how you report.

When filing your FAFSA, pay close attention to every question about your assets and income. This is important as you can legally exclude or omit specific income sources and assets you may own.

For example, you don't need to report any of the following assets:

- your primary residence,
- car,
- a boat you may own, or
- furniture in your home.

You also don’t have to report social security as income.

By mistakenly reporting these items on your FAFSA, you can unwittingly increase your EFC, thereby slashing your college financial aid.

So, be very cautious of the questions and what they say, and what they're asking for. Look closely at the assets and what you can and cannot submit.

Keep in mind that you can appeal your financial aid package. If you get your EFC back and don't like it, you will appeal it. Right?

If you had a substantial change to your financial aid, or if other schools have awarded you wildly different aid packages, it may be worth contacting the financial aid office.

Remember always to remain grateful and courteous while making a solid case for yourself.

Be prepared to provide supplemental documentation supporting your claim, as well as information requested by the school.

The financial aid process is a big one. Everyone must do it. Hopefully, they'll have some things you can do to maximize your financial aid. You can take these things and talk to your accountant or CPA.

Go to the financial aid website, read the fine print, and understand this process outside of what I just discussed.

Common Myths about FAFSA

Here are some myths about FAFSA:

Myth one: My family makes too much money for me to qualify for aid. Sometimes people say, "Well, we make too much money, so we don't even apply." That's not necessarily true. If you do make a lot of money and they say you don't qualify, apply for FAFSA anyway. Because it will also contribute and show up if you need to take out a student loan, still make sure you apply.

Myth two: I must file taxes before completing the federal student aid application.

That's another myth. Apply for FAFSA now, even if you're waiting to file your taxes. Get the process started. They will link up your past taxes. And when you do your upcoming taxes, it will link up again.

Myth three: The FAFSA is too hard to fill out.

That's a myth. It takes no more than about 21 minutes online and is probably faster than that now.

Myth four: My grades are not good enough to get aid.

As a high school student, qualifying for FAFSA isn't dependent on your grades. It's not about your academics; it's more about showing a need for money. So, be sure to apply for the aid.

Myth five: My ethnicity or age makes me ineligible for aid.

There is more that goes into the FAFSA process than your EFC versus your age and your ethnicity. So, make sure you apply.

Myth six: I support myself, so I don't have to include my parents' info on the FAFSA.

Even if you support yourself and there are some things you can do to be an independent student, guess what? There is still a lot that needs to be done where that is concerned.

Myth seven: I already completed the FAFSA once, so I don't need to complete it again.

That is not true. You must complete the FAFSA every year that you need the money. Every. Single. Year.

Myth 7.25: The FAFSA is only for grant money and scholarships.

That's not true, either. When you complete FAFSA, it does go towards helping you identify grants and scholarships. But if you need to take out a loan, they can easily calculate how much money you'll need to borrow, i.e., a parent loan, a student loan, and whatever goes along with that.

Understanding these myths will help you develop the most formidable and efficient plan to access the fund you need for your kids' college.

I have shared the most important ideas you need to get started. Take up the role and experience tremendous results.

If you need more help and clarity, I have more resources and advice in my College funding Course at KantisSimmons.com

USE THIS AREA TO JOT SOME NOTES AND YOUR ACTIVE CURRENT THOUGHTS ABOUT THIS SECTION

CHAPTER 5: THE "I"

INITIATE THE PROCESS

Chapter 5 – The "I"
INITIATE THE PROCESS

I have shown you how to develop your plan. But you need to know the best way you can utilize to kickstart the plan you've created.

I will be showing how to initiate the whole process in this chapter. Remember, the equation is GM + OM + YM.

GM is dealing with the government's money.

OM is other people's money.

..and lastly, YM is your money.

OM is other people's money, and it shows up through scholarships and loans.

I'm going to spend most of this chapter talking about scholarships.

Here's an excellent place to take notes; this will get good.

Here are 7.25 ways to locate college scholarships. You may wonder, "Why do I keep saying 7.25 ways?"

Well, I was born with a “cool birth defect.”

If you've heard or read about my story, you know I grew up feeling like I can't, I won't, I never. I had this finger mess because of my congenital disability.

One of the things my mom encouraged and taught me was, "Kantis, quit looking at what you don't have and focus on what you do have."

I want to say this to you now…

You can do this!,

Despite what you don't have in life - a relationship, money, or the feeling like you “haven't done right.” Don't focus on that; focus on what you do have.

Focus on this opportunity and how you can maximize where you are today.

So, when you see the number 7.25, know it comes from me having 7.25 fingers.

Guess what?

That didn't stop me from going to college, nor did it stop me from getting three college degrees. That didn't stop me from getting scholarships. I probably could have used it to get more scholarships (lol), and I'll tell you about that in this section.

Here are 7.25 ways to locate scholarships:

1. Look local
2. Look college
3. Look online
4. Look social
5. Look corporate
6. Look community
7. Look Greek
8. Look crowdfunding

Now I'm going to break all of this down.

#1 Look Local

"There's gold in your backyard."

Now, here's what I mean when I say look local.

Look local with your high school counselors and those in your current school. You don't know what you don't know.

So, what you want to do now is talk to your school's counselors. Talk to the teachers, the graduation coaches, to any and everybody in your local circle. Now here's a little trick about looking local.

Let's say you go to a school on the south side of the city, and you're looking local and talking to the teacher at your school. Who says you can't speak to the counselor or the graduation coach of the school on the north side? Did you catch that? Speak to other local counselors and coaches.

You may go to a school on the south side, but who says you can't talk to a counselor at another school? You may go to a school in the east, but who says you can't speak to somebody in the west?

Looking local; not only looking in your school but if you have connections, talk to counselors and individuals in other schools.

Let's just keep it real...

I live on the South side of Atlanta. I don't know all the schools on the South side of Atlanta. There are some other schools on the north side of Atlanta. Don't let the knowledge gap - what you don't know, stop you from reaching your goal! It may take the opportunity for you to have conversations with people who may know the ins and outs, the secrets about where the money is, and know how you can access it.

Never put everything in the hands of one person. So, look local. Talk to those you know locally and those you don't know locally.

#2 - Look, College

Seek college scholarships at your desired colleges.

Let's say, for example, you have dedicated time to apply to six colleges. You're interested in six colleges. Yeah, you put those six colleges on your FAFSA form, but I also want you to go and seek scholarships at those colleges in the admissions department and on the college website.

Speak with alums of that college.

Also, look to see if there are scholarships in the departments of the programs that you want to attend. So, look at the college.

Even before you get into the colleges, seek scholarships at that college, especially in the alum department. That's number two; look at college. Yes, there's a lot of information on the school's website, but you still have to look.

#3 - Look Online

"Seek, and you shall find."

Here's what I want you to do. This should become a part of your family night; you should do this.

When searching, enter your field of study, plus the word scholarship in google.

For instance, I'm going to type in physical therapy and then scholarship.

Notice, before I even hit return, Google already gives me some recommended places to look.

By typing in the word (your desired field of study) plus scholarship, I've been given suggestions about where to look.

physical therapy scholarship

physical therapy scholarship**s**
physical therapy scholarship**s 2021**
physical therapy scholarship**s for high school seniors**
physical therapy scholarship**s for minorities**
physical therapy scholarship**s for undergraduate students**
physical therapy scholarship**s for international students**
physical therapy scholarship**s philippines**
physical therapy scholarship**s and grants**
physical therapy scholarship **essay**
physical therapy scholarship **2020**

Google Search   I'm Feeling Lucky

Here are some examples:

- Physical therapy scholarships 2021.
- Physical therapy military scholarships.
- Physical therapy scholarships for minorities.
- Physical therapy scholarships and grants.

The system is giving me some recommended phrases.

For this example, I'm going to click "physical therapy scholarships for minorities."

Here's what's going to take place…

At the very top of Google, Yahoo and MSN, you will see ads wherever you decide to search. These ads are just listings of organizations that have paid money to ensure they stay at the top. The other links you'll see are links that people or websites have put out regarding scholarships.

Now, here's the cool thing I want you to do.

Do you see what you've searched for?

Do you see the websites down at the very bottom?

What you want to do is go down the rabbit trail.

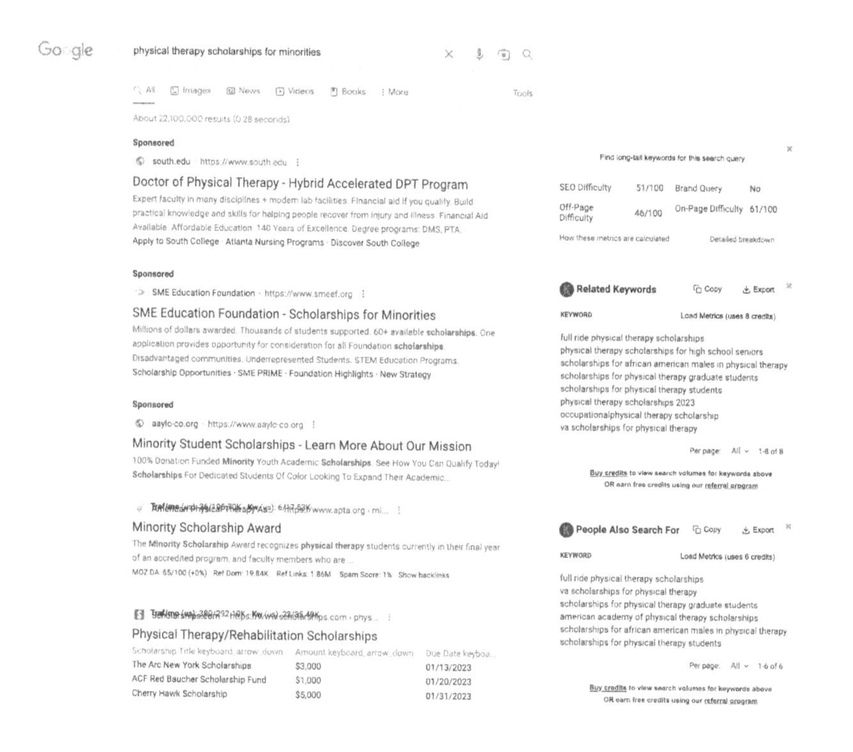

Click through the websites.

Look for scholarship requirements. Areas to search are personal essays, curriculum, and a completed application form.

You must go through and do your research.

You can take your field of study and do this all day and night.

Let me do it for Biology Scholarships…

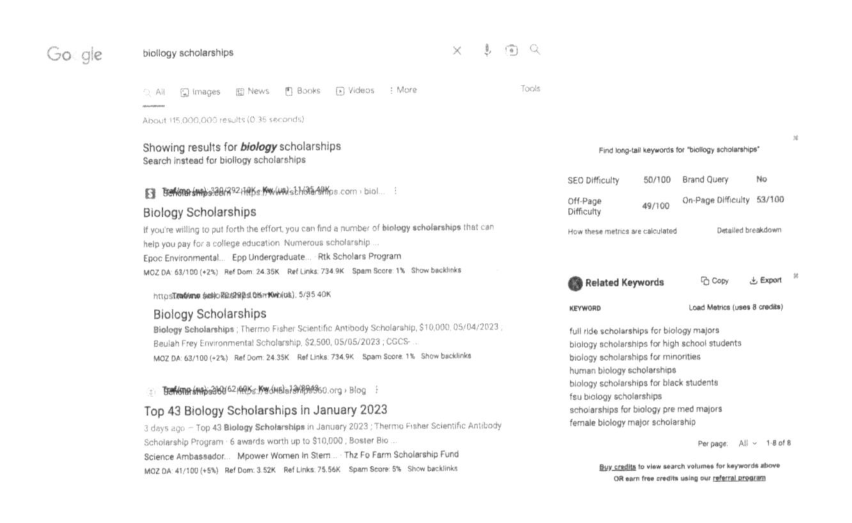

I didn't even spell the word correctly, and Google is giving me information on Biology scholarships. So, I can pick one. "Biology scholarships for high school students."

I've pulled up Biology scholarships at scholarships.com, and I see that the deadline has already passed for some, and dealing is approaching for others…

But then they offered $500, $800, and $40,000 scholarships. Who wouldn't want that?

You always want to look for what's required, such as the GPA and how much they pay.

Remember, it is GM plus OM plus YM; it's all adding up.

Grants are massive for those in graduate school.

People often ask me, "Hey, can you find a scholarship in graduate school?" Yes.

Take your 'field of study' plus the word 'grants', and go down the rabbit trail. It tells you what to expect, what's needed.

When I was looking for a sports medicine scholarship, Google gave me more suggested phrases - scholarship, sports medicine scholarships in Texas, Minnesota, American College, Winthrop University.

I spelled it wrong, but Google gave me everything I needed.

I also found some outdated scholarships, but if they gave out a scholarship in 2018, they would probably still be giving out that same one in 2021 or 2024.

I've found Music Production scholarships and other music scholarships for music majors in college.

You may already be in college, but you can still get a scholarship. They are scholarships for practically everything.

- Are you left-handed?
- Are you a mom?
- Are you a woman?
- Are you a high school senior?
- Are you an international student?
- Are you a Hispanic student?

- Do you have a birthmark?
- Do you have a birth defect or any other type of disability?
- Are you a single parent trying to return and get your degree?

Then, click and go down the rabbit trail.

I don't claim I have a disability; however, many of my friends and people I mentor have disabilities.

Let's say you're in medical school or doing social work and looking for scholarships. Chances are that you will get stingy and greedy with it when you know about this stuff. You won't want to tell anybody.

Anyway, I don't care what you're majoring in...I need you to search for it.

Also, another great keyword is 'fellowships'. I went to grad school and received two master's degrees because of fellowships

How do you tell if the scholarships are legitimate?

By going down the rabbit trail. By going through the process of calling and getting the application and applying.

#4 - Look Social

Next, look at social media.

Everybody's posting on social media.

Try using hashtags. People use hashtags all the time. As for me, I went to Instagram to see what popped up!

Everybody's using hashtags. You can see something pop up on Instagram and follow that, especially if it's relevant to you or someone you know. Take your phrase plus the word hashtag, and then follow the hashtags.#Yourfield

I've found Philippine scholarships or scholarships over in Poland. So, start following hashtags. Scholarships are available right now. You can even hashtag #music.

Here's a cool thing about this:

You can also go to pages and groups withing Facebook. There are Facebook pages that talk about specific scholarships.

Remember, take your phrase, use the word, and hashtag it.

I searched for sorority/fraternity scholarships and discovered that the Omega Psi Phi Fraternity gives a scholarship.

Follow the rabbit trail.

Don't just use social media to post selfies.

You can also go to Twitter and search.

I was banned on Twitter for a while, but after, it said, "Welcome back.".. I started searching for scholarships.

Scholarship info is abundant.

For example, hashtag #medicine, hashtag #scholarship, hashtag medicine, and now you can follow the rabbit trail.

You can search for how to find and win scholarships. You are using the tools that are shared to do your best work.

Can you do this?

Is this helpful?

Now you're using social media, not just to post about what you ate, where you're going, or pictures of yourself. But guess what? You are now using social media, using the internet to get information on scholarships.

#5 - Look Corporate

If you are a parent (or if your parent) is working a full-time job, you may have noticed that in your HR department, your company offers scholarships to the kids of the employees. At least some companies do.

For example, Coca-Cola has a fiscal budget of $30 million to run it's company for the year…

Let's say that for that year, Coca-Cola is only going to use $28 million from the $30 million that they had budgeted.

To stay within their fiscal budget, they now take the extra two million and give it towards scholarships (and good causes) rather than giving everyone raises.

I want you to look corporate.

Ask your grandmother, grandfather, uncle, aunt, or anybody who is working a corporate job to see if that corporation offers scholarship funding for the kids of those who work there.

Then go apply!

#6 - Look Community

Seek out organizations and associations that do what you desire to do.

Coca-Cola is an excellent scholarship. Why? They are looking for ways to help people. This is good.

Here's what I mean by looking at the community.

Have you ever walked into a doctor's office and noticed the degrees of that doctor on the wall?

Have you ever looked at those degrees?

Then, maybe next to the degrees, you will see some certificates.

Those certificates have names of organizations in which that doctor or entrepreneur worked.

Guess what?

Those sorts of organizations in the community give scholarships!

Here's what you want to do.

Let's say your son or daughter wants to go into the field of music. A good strategy is to try finding some music association or organization in your area.

Maybe you want to go into physical therapy or sociology or physiology or English, or Math. What organizations in your community, right around your neighborhood, right near where you live, offer scholarships? Look for them.

I remember clearly that when I was looking to go into Chemistry, the American Chemical Society had a state chapter. They have a regional branch and a national chapter. All that exists because it's an organization or association. Look there.

#7 - Look Greek

Now, you may have heard of Greek sororities or fraternities. Guess what?

They are not all about step shows and having good times. No, they are in it to support community efforts.

I received a scholarship from Delta Sigma Theta and Alpha Kappa Alpha, and I'm all male.

Neither sorority said I had to be a female to apply for or receive their scholarships. So, I applied for both.

I got an Omega Psi Phi scholarship.

I got an Alpha Phi Alpha scholarship. I

think I got a Sigma scholarship, also.

I'm talking $1,000 here, $2,000 there, $3,000 there, $1,500 there, and $500 there.

GM plus OM plus YM was how I paid for college, and you can do the same.

#7.25 - Look Crowdfunding

Last but not least, look at crowdfunding.

What does that mean?

Pass the offering bucket.

If you've been to a church, you've probably seen them pass the offering bucket, right?

Crowdfunding is where you can build a website, a crowdfunding website.

You Google crowdfunding, and they'll give you a web page, and you state the 'cause' or the need for this website.

You can say, "Hey, my son Johnny wants to be a veterinarian; who wants to help little horses with broken legs? It's his goal to do this…, this… and this. Then, start his own business and give back. Would you guys be open to helping little Johnny find the money for college?"

Now aunts, uncles, and friends have a link to send money to that crowdfunding page.

My advice is not just to say, "Hey, I need scholarship money," but to attach the scholarship to a great need or a great mission. A mission-driven crowdfunding page gets the most money. People will now donate to the mission so that this individual can fulfill the mission.

That's another way to get access to scholarships, by "passing the offering bucket" and doing crowdfunding.

Here are a few additional places you can search for scholarships

- Scholly,
- College Board Scholarship Search,

- Fastweb,
- scholarshipsearch.com,
- Cappex,
- SHEG,
- Niche,
- Petersons,
- Department of Labor.

These are search engines.

You can go in, go to these pages and search all day. They're a lot like Google apps. If you have an iPhone or an Android, there are so many apps to find scholarships in your hand.

Here are the topapps that I recommend for college-bound students and families

1. ScholarshipOwl,
2. RaiseMe,
3. College Scholarships,

4. PLEXUSS,
5. Scholly,
6. HBCU HUB,
7. College Scholarship Calculator,
8. Scholarships.com
9. Fastweb,
10. CollegeHunch

Now, all of this can be overwhelming. My recommendation is to get a scholarship organized. How do you get scholarship-organized?

- Get the scholarship name.
- Get the scholarship organization.
- Get the scholarship requirements.
- Get the scholarship contact info.
- Get the scholarship due date.
- Get the scholarship link.

This can be overwhelming, but you've got to get organized.

Lastly, use an excel file or download the worksheet that comes with my scholarship and college funding course (see KantisSimmons.com). Use it to break down the scholarship name, the organization, the requirements, the scholarship due date, and the link. Have this document and get organized. When you find something, you fill in the contact info, the requirements, and the amount of money and then check it off.

Put skin in the game.

If you want a return, you've got to work.

Again, here are the 7.25 ways to locate scholarships:

1. look local,
2. look college,
3. look online,
4. look social,
5. look corporate,

6. look community,
7. look Greek, and
8. look crowdfunding.

These are the ways you initiate the process.

Now you understand the process, but you have to initiate it.

Was this helpful for you? Are you going to do it?

CHAPTER 6: THE "N"

NAIL DOWN SCHOLARSHIPS

Chapter 6 – The “N”
NAIL DOWN SCHOLARSHIPS

You can locate scholarships all day long, but it’s more important to land them.

The first thing you did was focus on your future.

Now, you understand the process.

You've named your goal.

You've developed a plan.

You've initiated the process.

After all that, the next thing is to nail down scholarships.

I will share the tips on how you can nail scholarships below:

Fill out applications

First and foremost, you have to fill out the applications.

You can't win the lottery if you don't buy a ticket. You can't get a scholarship if you don't fill out a scholarship application. So, that's number one when nailing down a scholarship.

Increase your marketability

Be different, be memorable.

When you have an opportunity to apply for a scholarship, whether there's an opportunity on the application or in the essay, you need to increase your marketability.

Here's what I mean…

The scholarship may say that you are required to have a 3.5 GPA.

Well, guess what?

Everybody who has applied for the scholarship has a 3.5 GPA. But honestly, you're in the marketing business.

How can you stand out on your application?

How can you stand out in your essays?

How can you be different?

How can you be memorable so that your application or essay jumps off the page and they remember you?

Share your story

Let them see the real you. Whether in person or on the application or essay, show them the real you.

You might have had a hard time in one of the classes or your grades dropped, maybe in one semester.

Let's say you had a death in your family, and because of that death, your grades dropped, let them see that and express the real you.

"Hey, I went through this. I lost focus. I was down, but things came back up. But you know what? My grandmother, who died, impressed upon me the importance of attending college and reaching my goals as a therapist. And I want to make my grandmother happy and keep her legacy going. So, would you give me a scholarship?"

Let them see the real you.

Show them what you're about because our world loves a good story.

Let them see the real you.

Diversify your interests

Look outside the box.

For example, let's say you want to go into Chemistry. Look outside the box and look for STEM scholarships.

Maybe you want to go into Music. Look outside the box and consider Music Production scholarships.

Perhaps you want to go into business. Look outside the box and consider an Accounting scholarship.

Look outside the box. Diversify your interests.

- Academics?
- Extracurricular activities?

- Left-handed?
- Birth defect?

Think outside the box!

Now, the goal is to use all of this to create a total picture of who you are, what you're about, and how you can serve them. show them how they can invest in you.

Recycle & reuse your recommendations & essays

I want you to get recommendations from people who know you, form teachers, coaches, and counselors.

And when you're looking for a recommendation, do not wait until the last minute to ask for one. Why? Because they have a lot of other people who want recommendations, as well. So, get those requests for recommendations in early.

In some cases, with scholarship forms or even college applications, they want the recommendations to come directly from the person who wrote them.

So, ensure your teacher, your counselor, or whomever it may be, has all the information needed to email or mail it off. Let them know where to go with those recommendations.

You may have a recommendation that you used for a college application. If it'll work, reuse that recommendation for a scholarship application. If you have an essay for college applications, you can also use it for a scholarship application.

Maybe you're applying for three scholarships. If one essay works for the other scholarship applications, then reuse it. If you need to tweak parts of it, so it speaks the language needed for the new application, recycle and reuse. This process can be tedious, but if you can, recycle and reuse, and know where to go and maneuver it.

Get those grades up

Nobody wants to buy an ugly truck.

Here is the thing that I want you to realize: when colleges, organizations, groups, sororities, fraternities, local community groups, grandmothers, grandfathers, aunts, uncles, and church members invest in you, they want a return on their investments.

You have invested your time and your money to go through this book. So you expect a return.

When people invest scholarship money in you, they want a return.

They want a return of excellence.

They want a return of awesomeness.

They want to see and say, "Wow, we supported this person, and now look at what they've done with their career and life!"

And I believe one of the best ways to do that, foundationally, is to get your grades up.

Get it done. Be that person.

You won't always be in school, college, or grad school. But while you're there, play your A-game and get those grades up.

Let Your Light Shine

Here's another thing, let your light shine.

Bring your personality and passion to the interview.

Now, I always recommend, if you can, when you visit a college and when you can interview for a scholarship, to let your light shine. Let your light shine, whether in person, virtual or even over the phone.

"This little light of mine, I'm going to let it shine."

Let your personality and your passion shine.

I believe that you attract what you give off.

If you give off poison, toxic behavior, or an unhealthy attitude, I believe you'll attract that.

So, in your applications, interviews, and essays, let your personality shine. Let them see the real you. Let them see the best part of you.

Again, if you've had some downtimes in your academic career and life, talk about it. Guess what? Everybody has had one downtime or the other. We've all failed a course or two. It's not the end of the world. Let your light shine.

Real people with real emotions are reading those essays. And you have got to have the correct information to guide you on how best you can write your essays to reach the hearts of those who read them.

Tips to Write An Excellent Essay

#1 - the title of your essay.

The title of your essay leads to them reading the first line of your essay. A great first line of your essay leads them to read the first paragraph of your essay. The first paragraph of your essay leads them to read the entire essay.

Now, what if you have a whack title? It will most likely not catch their attention to read the first line.

If the first line of your essay is not engaging, maybe they won't be intrigued to read the first paragraph.

If the first paragraph is not as engaging, they probably won't read or even open the whole essay.

Now here's something I want you to do. I want you to take an assessment. I want you to do 10 and 10. I want you to write down 10 accomplishments you've had in school.

Maybe you received a music award. Perhaps you're the Student Government president. Maybe you got the highest GPA. Maybe you're the first one to go to college. Perhaps you're in the science club, maybe out of a foster home, maybe you serve in the foster home. Perhaps you are an award recipient in your community.

Write down 10 of your accomplishments. Then, look at the stories and setbacks.

What are some unique stories you have?

What are some setbacks you have had?

For example, I never really used it, but I could have: I was born with a birth defect. That was a story; you could call it a setback. I can type faster than most people. There's nothing I can't do. I played baseball. There are lots of things I can do. The only thing I can't do is wear a winter glove on my hand. I can wear winter mittens. Somebody wanted to buy me some mittens. I'm like, "Don't buy me mittens. That's embarrassing. A grown man wearing mittens." That's funny. Lol

Another setback could be that your grandmother encouraged you to advance your degree. Maybe you had a grandmother, a parent, or somebody close to you die. That was a setback that you can turn into a story.

Something like your desire to work on cars and airplanes… that's a story.

My parents met during their freshman year in college. That's a story.

Not sure what to major in, death in the family, or injury; you can talk about that where it's relevant.

So, I want you to take the assessments of yourself, your accomplishments, stories, and setbacks.

Write down

- your top 10 accomplishments (with stories)
- Your top 10 setbacks 9with stories)

List them out because now this will give you the content for your essays.

I want you to add a verb to it. That's 10 times 10, plus a verb.

This is a nice little trick. Anytime you go into an interview, try to sell yourself. If you get the chance to talk to somebody, then market yourself. Whether you're doing any of that or getting in with the professor or an organization, you will need to use verbs.

"I raised, I led, I started, I mentored, I created, I discovered, I initiated."

You take those verbs, and now you add them to your 10 accomplishments.

Take those verbs, and add them to your 10 stories. Verb plus your 10 times 10.

Also, always try to get recommendations. I mentioned this earlier, get them from teachers, advisors, counselors, mentors, and friends who know you. Don't try to get them from teachers with whom you don't have a rapport. Talk to people who know you.

If you are a Chemistry major, here's another tip to land a scholarship.

Look for STEM scholarships.

Look for Science scholarships.

Look for Pre-Med scholarships.

Look for Biology scholarships.

You can have a Biology scholarship but still major in something else. You can have a STEM or science scholarship and major in one of the Sciences.

For example, if you are a Music major, look for Arts, entertainment, and Performance scholarships. Speech Pathology major? Consider Radio,

Journalism, and Communications scholarships. Then, speak that lingo to land those scholarships!

Don't hide your poor grades; talk about them. Talk about what you learned from them.

You may have questions about weighted versus unweighted grades based on the field of study you're going into. For example, if you're going into an Engineering field, they will look at those Science and Math course grades.

Here are some more tips on writing essays.

Write essays about something important to you.

It could be an experience, a person, a book, or anything that has impacted your life. Something important.

Don't just recount your stories or setbacks; reflect on them. Anyone can write about how they won the big game or the summer they spent in Rome. When recalling these events, you must give more than a play-by-play or itinerary. Please describe what you learned from the experience and how it changed you. Don't just recount; reflect on it. Show rather than merely tell.

Being funny in your essays is tough, but try it.

A student who can make an admissions officer or scholarship coordinator laugh is rare. You don't get lost in the shuffle. But beware. What you think is funny and what an adult working in a college thinks is funny are probably different. I caution you against one-liners and anything off-color. So, be careful when you use specific phrases.

When writing an essay, **start early and write several drafts**.

Never, ever send in your first draft. Write it, then set it aside. You go to sleep and let the essay sleep. Then, days later, review that essay. Reread it. Put yourself in the shoes of the reader.

Is the essay interesting?

Does the essay flow logically with a sense of good cadence?

Does it reveal something about the applicant that is interesting?

Is it written in the applicant's voice?

So, please write an essay; let it sit; let it breathe. And then, go back and also submit some different drafts.

No repeats.

What you write in your application essay or personal statement should not contradict any other part of your application, nor should it repeat itself.

This isn't the place to list your awards or discuss your grades or test scores.

Here's what I mean…

If you talked about your grades and test scores on your application, don't just mention them again; reflect upon them. Don't just repeat what they just saw in your application. Reflect, grow from it, and then take it to the next level.

Answer the questions being asked in your essays. Avoid reusing an answer to a similar question from another application. I know that earlier, I mentioned reusing and recycling. But only reuse and recycle the things that fit.

If that essay does not ask for that, don't put it in it. Answer the question that is being asked.

Review and reread.

Write an essay and let your teachers or colleagues read it before sending it off. Check it, triple-check it.

Make sure your grammar and your spelling are up to par. We're humans, so there are certain things that we tend to miss.

Make sure you put some other eyes on it, like your teachers or counselors.

Have people read it and give you their perspectives to make it better.

Lastly, here's one last thing to consider when writing your essay. **Consider why their university is excellent to attend** and why they should invest in you. These are two things that you can easily talk about in your essays.

Has this been helpful with nailing down scholarships?

If yes, put yourself to work, and nail yours soon.

USE THIS AREA TO JOT SOME NOTES AND YOUR ACTIVE CURRENT THOUGHTS ABOUT THIS SECTION

CHAPTER 7: THE "G"

GET AND KEEP THE

MONEY

Chapter 7 – The "G"
GET AND KEEP THE MONEY

Congratulations on reaching the final chapter of Scholarship Secrets Revealed!

By now, you have gained valuable insight and strategies to help you navigate the process of finding and securing funding for your higher education goals.

In this final chapter, we will delve into the importance of understanding what is required to get and keep your scholarship and how to approach the process of reapplying if necessary.

First and foremost, it's crucial to understand the requirements for obtaining and maintaining your scholarship.

Here are a few keys to getting and keeping scholarships:

Understand what is required to get the scholarship

- Must you have a certain GPA?
- Do you have to participate in a particular major?
- Do you have to participate in the marching band?
- Do you have to participate in the glee club?
- What's required to get the scholarship?
- What's the recommendation like?
- What's the application like?

We've talked about all those things, so find out what is required.

Once you get it, what is required to keep it?

- Does your GPA have to be at a certain level?
- Do you have to do so many hours of research?
- What GPA is required to stay in good standing?

I've known people who had scholarships and lost them because their grades dropped. And they might've been on probation for a semester and had the opportunity to get their grades back up to be in right standing.

Is this a one-time offer or a year-to-year offer?

When you apply for scholarships, they will tell you if it's just for one year.

I saw a scholarship for $50,000, and they broke it up in increments of 10,000 over four to five years. That is a year-to-year offer.

Or you can apply for a scholarship, and you're only eligible for that one semester or that one year.

Typically, they are yearly, not just for one semester.

Then, you want to find out what is required to reapply. Whom can you talk to about reapplying, if needed?

1. What's required to get it?
2. What's required to keep it?
3. What GPA is required to hold on to it?
4. Is this a one-time offer?
5. Is it a year-to-year offer?
6. Whom can I talk to about reapplying, if needed?

Now, if you're in a situation where you need to get more scholarships, do everything I've said in the other parts of this program.

If you don't have the money for school, your number one job should be looking for money for school. It becomes part of your habit. Because, if not, on the back end, you'll be paying student loans.

Do the work now, so you don't have to do the job and pay people later. Do as much as you possibly can.

Remember the equation: GM + OM + YM.

And finally, don't be afraid to ask questions.

It's essential to be proactive and seek answers to any questions about the scholarship process.

Whether you're inquiring about the requirements for obtaining or maintaining a scholarship or asking about the possibility of obtaining multiple scholarships, asking the right questions can make all the difference.

Is it okay to get multiple scholarships? Find out.

"Hey, do you have a scholarship for me now; can I get multiple scholarships?"

Ask those questions.

"Hey, can this be sent to my home, or can this be sent to the school?"

Ask those questions. What's required?

If you find yourself in a situation where you need to secure additional scholarships, remember to follow the strategies outlined in this book.

This includes focusing on your future, understanding the process, naming your goals, developing a plan, and initiating the process.

It's important to make finding funding for your education a top priority, as taking on student loans can be a burden in the long run.

I hope that the knowledge and strategies shared in this book have equipped you with the tools you need to confidently navigate the process of finding and securing funding for your higher education.

Remember to stay focused on your goals, and research, and be proactive in seeking opportunities.

You can achieve your dreams of obtaining a college scholarship with the right mindset and approach.

USE THIS AREA TO JOT SOME NOTES AND YOUR ACTIVE CURRENT THOUGHTS ABOUT THIS SECTION

SCHOLARSHIP SECRETS

NEXT STEPS

Conclusion

Congratulations! You have reached the end of Scholarship Secrets Revealed.

You are now equipped with all the knowledge and tools you need to make your higher education dreams a reality.

With the tips and strategies outlined in this book, you can confidently seek, find, gain and keep scholarships for your college education.

Throughout this journey, you have learned about the importance of understanding the process, setting clear goals, developing a solid plan, initiating the process, and nailing down the scholarship.

These steps will guide you on your path to success and help you reach your career destination through higher education.

In addition to providing you with the skills and mindset you need to succeed, this book has also given you a detailed overview of the nationwide educational and scholarship landscape.

You now have a deep understanding of the various options available to you and how to navigate the process with grace, confidence, and unwavering assurance that you will get the scholarship you need.

Don't forget that this book is your companion on this journey.

Feel free to refer back to it often as you progress through the process of seeking and securing scholarships.

With the information and guidance provided on these pages, you are well on your way to success.

I am thrilled to have been able to share my knowledge and experience with you, and I hope that you will apply these tips to the letter.

I look forward to reading your success story and hearing about all the fantastic things you will accomplish with your higher education.

Until then, keep pushing forward and never give up on your dreams!

For more information and resources on how to pay the college tuition bill, visit

KANTISSIMMONS.COM

ABOUT KANTIS SIMMONS

Kantis Simmons is a highly regarded author, speaker, and former NASA scientist dedicated to ending the academic failure epidemic, reducing teacher turnover rates, and tackling the trillion-dollar student loan debt crisis affecting schools, colleges, and families across America.

Simmons has personally experienced the transition from high school to college and graduate school and knows what it takes to pay for tuition through scholarships. In fact, he funded his education entirely through scholarships.

Now, Simmons is helping thousands of families offset college tuition costs and pay their bills through college scholarships. Through his book, Scholarship Secrets Revealed, he hopes to share his knowledge and experience with others and show them how to graduate debt-free.

Printed in the USA
CPSIA information can be obtained
at www.ICGtesting.com
BVHW051622230823
668815BV00004B/29